Winning Bowls

Winning Bowls

**An introduction to Crown Green Bowls
by Chris Mills**

Editor of *Bowls International*

W. Foulsham & Co. Ltd.
London · New York · Toronto · Cape Town
Sydney

W. Foulsham & Company Limited
Yeovil Road, Slough, Berkshire, SL1 4JH

ISBN 0-572-01219-5

Photoset and printed in Great Britain by Rowland
Phototypesetting Limited and St Edmundsbury Press
Bury St Edmunds, Suffolk

Contents

Chapter 1

The history of the game

The Ancient Egyptians left behind one of the seven 'wonders of the world' as a memory of their culture. What many people may not know is that they probably invented the game that today delights adherents both in the UK and in many other countries of the world – the game of bowls.

The early game was played with 'skittles' and rounded stones and was later adopted by other early civilisations in China, Greece and Rome. Inevitably it was brought into Europe and from there it was but a short step to Britain.

One of the first recorded references to the game in Britain must surely be that uttered by King John – a monarch who had quite a few problems in his seventeen-year reign. 'Talk not of bowls. What is life but a game of bowls in which the King is all too frequently knocked down.'

Bowls therefore rivals archery as the grandparent of all English sports and it was that fact which also made it the curse of many kings. At times, they even saw the sport as a threat to the existence of their country because it encouraged people to abandon their archery practice to play. And until the advent of gunpowder the archer was an important man in his country's defence.

In the summer of 1588 all England awaited the long-prepared blow of the Spanish Armada. For three years Philip of Spain had been building a fleet that would bring his enemies to their knees. One day a ship's boat sailed into Plymouth with the news that this mighty fleet of warships had been sighted off the Isles of Scilly.

Second-in-command of the English fleet was a well-known admiral, Sir Francis Drake. Along with other officers he was engaged that day in a game of bowls. When his colleagues made moves to join their boats he rebuked them with – 'there's plenty of time yet to win this game and thrash the Spaniards too.' Legend has it that Drake lost his game of bowls which perhaps accounts for the reason the Spaniards suffered so much afterwards! This still remains one of the most famous bowls matches of all time.

William Shakespeare lived about the same time, and his plays include a number of references to the game. Perhaps one of the best known appears in *Richard II* when the Queen and two ladies are strolling in the Duke of York's garden. The Queen remarks, 'What sport shall we devise here in this garden to drive away the heavy thought of care?', to

It looks as though we will have to replay this end, Sir Francis.

which one of the ladies replies, 'Madam, shall we play bowls.' 'Twill make one think the world is full of rubs and that my fortune runs against the bias,' the Queen replies.

That statement points to a dramatic change in the game. Until that time bowls had been perfectly round, usually made of oak wood and about 14 cm (5½ inches) in diameter. But the reference to bias clearly indicates that these bowls were now loaded or shaped in such a way that they would turn as they slowed down on their delivery path.

Apart from the private games enjoyed by the aristocracy, the game of bowls had a very bad reputation because of its association with ale houses and gambling dens. More recently many Crown greens were connected with public houses and inns, which had created the greens for their customers.

It has often been said that crown green bowls evolved because there are no flat and level areas of land in the north-west of England so it was necessary to devise a game of bowls that took this into account. And in fact no one is quite sure where the idea of the 'crown' originated, but it is created by the fact that the green rises from the edges to the centre anything from 15 to 45 cm (6 to 18 inches) – or even more in some extreme cases.

In the late 1880s the game began to get organised. Lancashire formed their own county organisation in 1888. At first this included Cheshire, but that county broke away to form their own association in 1910. Yorkshire (1892), Warwickshire and Worcester (1897), and Derbyshire (1909) followed.

The game's ruling body became the Crown Green Association, which was formed in 1907 and continued to look after the interests of amateurs until 1929 when Lancashire withdrew because they had professionals operating within their county. Their withdrawal led to Lancashire forming the National Crown Green Association which attracted Derbyshire and Cheshire but only lasted for five years.

Meanwhile, parks bowling was flourishing, and in 1911 the British Parks Association was formed in Manchester and has continued without a break ever since, although it is not a nationally recognised governing body.

Professionalism proved something of a problem for years, but in 1908 the Lancashire Professional Bowling Association – now the British PBA – was formed. A merger between the British and National associations brought some peace to the scene in 1932 and a year later the laws of the game were finalised and lodged at Stationer's Hall.

To protect their interests and give themselves a bigger platform, the CGBA changed their name to the British Crown Green Bowling Association at a meeting in Manchester on 1 December 1935. The authority now has 14 affiliated county associations and has been particularly successful in obtaining sponsorship and television coverage for the game. There has also been a significant increase in the number of crown green bowlers over the last five years, particularly amongst younger players.

The crown green game is mainly singles with each player having two bowls, although there are an increasing number of pairs competitions. Tournaments abound, many carrying substantial prizes. The most famous of these is the Waterloo Handicap played at the Waterloo Hotel in Blackpool. Despite higher prize money at other events, no tournament has yet rivalled the Waterloo's magical appeal. Blackpool's famous Mecca has also attracted many other major competitions.

Originally the prerogative of the north-west, the Midlands and west Yorkshire, crown green bowling is now attracting a much wider audience with new greens being opened in areas where this type of bowling was previously unknown.

_____

Chapter 2

So now you want to play?

Let's begin by dispensing with one of the biggest myths that has surrounded the game of bowls for such a long time – that it is purely 'an old man's game'. While it is true that there are many senior citizens who enjoy the game, there are now more and more young players coming into the sport – and picking up some top trophies too!

So whether you have just heard about the game from friends, seen some of the growing number of programmes offered to bowls enthusiasts on television or just watched bowlers in the local park, you now fancy having a go yourself. The simplest thing is to go along to a local club, find the club's secretary or any other official, and introduce yourself. The crown green outdoor season runs from the middle of March until the end of October, although there are some hardy winter bowling clubs.

If you don't fancy going to a recognised club straight away this doesn't prevent you beginning to play the game. There are many parks with municipal greens where you could play. And at moderate cost they will provide you with bowls, a jack and a mat.

Bowls
Before you really get into the game it is important to know something about the game and your tools of the trade – the bowls and jack. You will often hear players refer to the bowls as 'woods'. This is because until recent years they were mainly produced from a very hard wood, called lignum vitae, which comes from tropical countries. But like a lot of things this beautiful wood, so heavy that it has the rare quality

in that it sinks in water, has become very scarce and expensive and manufacturers have turned to cheaper substitutes based on plastic compounds.

Many players still seek out the old 'lignums' preferring to use them because of their so called 'live' running qualities. Funnily enough one of the rare sources of wooden bowls these days are from their flat green counterparts, who are discarding lignums in favour of composition bowls. That's not to say that composition bowls aren't gaining ground in the crown green world. Their main qualities being that they are rarely damaged, require little attention and should remain true-running longer.

In the crown green game, whether it be singles or pairs, each player uses two bowls. These bowls come in a variety of qualities, sizes, weight and bias – the most popular being one of two full bias and weighing anything from 1.2 to 1.4 kg (2 lb 10 oz to 3 lb).

Bias

There have been many attempts at giving a clear cut definition of the term 'bias'. Simply it is the tendency of a bowl to divert from a straight line in movement because of an imbalance built in by shaping. The degree to which a bowl will 'turn' depends on its shape – not any such in-built devices as lead weights! If you hold a bowl up and look at it you will see that one side of the bowl, which will always be the inner edge whichever side (or hand) you bowl on, is turned down slightly more than the other edge. This shaping effect is achieved on a lathe in the case of wooden bowls, but in the case of composition is built into the shape of the moulding.

Crown green bowls may be stamped 'two full', '2¼', '2½' and so on with '¼' increases up to four. The player therefore has a great choice of bowls and may find it an advantage to have several sets of different bias for all types of green.

13

In general terms, the higher the crown of the green the more heavily biased a bowl is used. Most players, however, use the 'two full' bowl to correspond with the jack.

The jack in crown green bowls corresponds in shape and bias to the bowls except that it is much smaller. In most cases this jack will be one that is approved by the British Crown Green Bowling Association and the British Parks Bowling Association. The correct measurements of these are contained in the 'Laws of the Game' at the back of this book but the important thing to remember is that they will be 'two full'.

The delivery of the jack plays a very important part in the crown green game. As it is biased a player will gain information about the running qualities of the green by observing its travel over the green.

All bowls have some indication of which is the bias side. This can be by a disc or by coloured rings, the larger rings indicating the non-bias side. It has always been a standing joke within the game of bowls that the only information you need to know to play is that 'the big rings are on the outside, the smaller ones on the inside'.

If you are a right-handed player and hold the bowl with the smaller rings nearest to your thumb, it will tend to turn to the right when delivered. This is known as sending the bowl on a 'thumb peg'. The opposite grip with the smaller rings or hollow disc to the left, is known as 'finger peg'.

Bowls will always try and turn in the direction of the bias but it must be remembered in crown green bowls that both the bias and the slope of the green cause the bowls to run in curved paths. The bias on a particular bowl remains unchanged, but the slope of the green may vary with each shot. The green will always tend to pull the bowl in the direction of the downward slope. As the player has the choice of which side he will use his bias, the dual effects of bias and green can be used together, widely curving the path of the bowl or making it run more or less straight.

A bowl will never run absolutely straight because as it slows down the effect of any bias becomes more pronounced and the bowl will curve in response to the bias.

When the bowl is held with the bias turned towards the centre or the crown of the green it is termed 'straight peg'. When the bowl is held on the side away from the crown it is called 'round peg'. In a straight peg shot, the slope of the green and the bias of the bowl are used in opposition to one another with the effect that the bowl runs almost straight. In a round peg shot, the slope of the green and the bias are used together to increase the curvature of the path of the bowl.

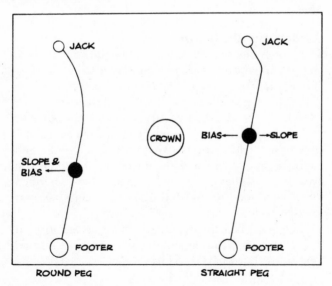

Straight peg bowling being the straightest way to the jack is the easiest to play and therefore used more by beginners, but all good players have to perfect round peg shots as without them a player will not get very far.

Treads

As well as the bias shaping of a bowl a further factor that can affect the running will be the width of the sole of the bowl – that is the part of the bowl that comes in contact with the green – which can be narrow, medium or broad. The scientific merits of these three 'treads' may be superfluous to the beginner but basically a bowl with a narrow sole will run slightly straighter and some say further because there is less of the bowl to 'grip' the green. There is also the additional factor of those players with small hands finding the narrow sole bowl easier to grip than a broader based bowl.

Learning about the game

Obviously the first thing for any beginner to do is to get involved with bowlers and seek their advice. There are always experienced bowlers who are prepared to offer advice on all aspects of the game.

When you are starting up, you will probably be able to borrow a set of bowls from the clubhouse for you to try before you decide to take the plunge and acquire your own set. It is not necessary when you first begin to have a brand new set, there are often some very good second-hand sets to be purchased at moderate cost.

The best place to acquire knowledge is of course at a bowls club, although many players have started out on the local parks greens.

Chapter 3

Making a start

Having decided to go along to a local club or park it's as well to know something about the green that you are going to play on. The size of a crown green varies for there is no official ruling on minimum or maximum dimensions. You may find yourself on a green 27 metres (30 yards) square or one even 55 metres (60 yards) square – and they're not always square either.

The term 'crown green' comes from the fact that the green rises from the edges to the centre of the green anything from 15 to over 50 centimetres (6 to over 20 inches). This rise isn't easily visible, but soon makes itself apparent when you are bowling!

The jack and the footer

Assuming that you have obtained a set of bowls, the next two 'tools of the trade' that you will require for a game are a jack and a 'footer'.

A crown green jack corresponds in shape and bias to the bowls, but is much smaller. The delivery of the jack is an important part of the crown green game because as it runs over the surface the player can gain much information about the shape and irregularities of the green by watching its movements.

The British Crown Green Bowling Association and the British Parks Bowling Association have adopted a standard two full bias jack used in all competitions which have their approval.

The footer is a small round mat on which the player must place his toe when bowling either jack or bowl. It should have a diameter of not less than 13 cm (5 inches) and not more than 15 cm (6 inches).

When delivering from the footer the player must have the same toe on the mat corresponding with his delivery arm (i.e. if he is right-handed, then his right toe must remain on the mat until the bowl has left his hand). A player must also bowl with the same hand throughout the game. The player also has possession of the footer until his bowl comes to rest.

Bowling techniques

In the previous chapter we talked about the effects of bias and the crown of the green and I think it's as well now to introduce the techniques of grip, stance and delivery.

Beginners who are anxious to improve their play should never hesitate to seek the advice of experienced players or just study them when they are playing. This is one of the ways for a novice to develop his skill. You should observe, and then try to emulate, the outstanding points in others' style of play, always bearing in mind that success in bowls is only achieved by regular and determined practice.

Grip

There are basically two classic grips in the game of bowls – the 'claw' and the 'cradle' – all others being a combination of the two. The claw grip is generally favoured in crown green game where the bowls are smaller and consequently easier to hold.

In the claw grip the bowl is placed firmly in the palm of the hand with the middle fingers spread out under the bowl, while the thumb and little finger give additional support on the side. The little finger is just level with the bottom of the disc and the thumb over the upper part or just above the large disc. The bowl need only be gripped sufficiently to prevent it slipping at the moment of delivery.

In the cradle grip the bowl just rests in the hand with the supporting fingers closer together than the claw and the thumb much lower at the side of the bowl. To prevent the bowl from slipping out of the hand during the backswing of delivery, the wrist is slightly cupped.

How you grip a bowl is largely the choice of the individual. The larger the size of your hand, the more choice you have in the manner with which you grip the bowl. The cradle grip tends to be used more by those with a small hand and sometimes by those players who prefer short marks.

Stance and delivery

It is very difficult to be specific about stance and delivery. The textbook will always teach you to be graceful and smooth with your movements and it is true that the better bowlers are those with a firm purposeful backswing and smooth follow-through. But many bowlers with unorthodox deliveries have been successful.

There are basically two stances – the upright and the crouch. Those players who adopt the upright stance have the advantage of starting from a well balanced position with a clear view of the jack. Throughout the movement from the preliminary address to the actual point of delivery there is a concentrated harmony of muscular action. The vital follow-through of the arm is reinforced by the whole weight of the body – a great help on heavy greens where you need a 'bit of push' to get the bowl moving.

As the hand passes backward for the commencement of the swing, the player rises on his toes and as he swings his arm, he bends his knees and, in the case of a right-handed player, steps forward on his left foot. The right hand and arm will follow through in a forward and upward motion, and after the bowl has left the hand a player may follow his bowl up the green for some distance.

In the crouch position the bowl will be delivered more directly at green level with less backswing and not such a pronounced follow-through. This stance is usually adopted by older or less agile players.

The crown green delivery is more of a semi-circular arm swing which is very useful on damp, heavy greens and for general long length play as this fuller swinging motion gives a greater impetus on delivery.

One of the main points with delivery is always to be natural in what you do. You will soon develop an automatic delivery which will give you a good control of length.

One point that is important – never be in a rush. That slight pause before your delivery will help your concentration and get you properly balanced.

Chapter 4

The shots of the game

Most of the games played in crown green bowls are singles, although pairs bowling is now gaining in popularity. In singles you will obviously either be bowling or watching your opponent. In crown green watching the performance of your opponent's bowls is very important.

Watching your opponent

When you are not leading the jack, always stand about a metre behind and about a metre to one side of whichever hand your opponent uses. There are three good reasons for doing this: to see the bias; to see the land over which the jack travels; and to observe your opponent's stance and delivery.

Although he usually will, your opponent is not obliged to tell you what bias or peg (finger or thumb) he is using when delivering the jack. He must, however, show you the jack. With time and experience, and certainly on your own green, you would be able to tell which peg had been played without looking at the jack.

You need to adopt a good position to observe the path of the jack so that you can pick out the strength or weight at which it has been delivered. But possibly the most important reason for standing back and to one side is the opportunity it gives you of observing your opponent's feet on the mat.

The rules dictate that a right-handed bowler must have his right foot on the mat, and vice versa with the left-hander, but this position can be varied. This will enable the player to vary the land or path to the jack.

Aiming points

Before sending the jack to set a mark it is best to select an aiming point on the green. This might be an area of lighter or darker grass, a weed blemish or anything that can be fixed with the eye. Then when making your delivery aim the jack for your selected spot and endeavour to follow the same line with your bowls. Obviously if you choose a very recognisable spot, your opponent in a game would pick this up as well, but as you gain in experience you will pick smaller, less noticeable ones.

In fact few bowlers look the same distance down the green for a distinguishing mark over which the jack has passed, some take a point close to the mat, others several metres away. Choosing a point close to the footer has a disadvantage in that on delivery you would not be looking at the jack. A mark further up the green-line will enable you to see the jack, which helps to find both your direction and the right distance. There is, of course, a certain amount of guesswork involved as your bowls may be stronger or weaker in bias than the jack and you will therefore have to make some adjustments to your shot.

Good length bowling

Accurate judgement of distance and good length bowling are two of the fundamentals of success at bowls and the one is dependent on the other. A good bowler should be able to visualise from the mat the distance of the jack and make adjustments with his second bowl, if his first was short or through – that is, went past the jack – to put it right on target. This ability to put on or take off a metre of running only comes, of course, with practice.

If a player is continually playing short bowls he can counteract this by mentally measuring his deficiency and then doubling it in length. If he was two metres short of the jack, he should pick a point two metres behind it and play for that spot. If over-running the jack, try and reduce the length accordingly.

Length bowling on a crown green is particularly important as with the possibility of diagonal marks the variations in length are increased. To become a really first class player you have to be able to bowl all lengths.

Differing conditions will, of course, determine how much weight you will need to apply to your bowls. A well cut, very dry green will be much faster than a wet green. On the fast green you will not need to make too much adjustment in weight to achieve your extra length, on a wet and heavy green you may need to increase your backswing to achieve the same result.

If the jack is delivered with the bias in favour of the slope of the green it will swing in a wide arc, known as round peg. But if the jack is bowled with the bias against the slope of the green then it will travel straight, or if the green has a large crown the jack may fall against the bias.

When bowling on a fast green no attempt should be made to go straight peg if an opponent has led with the jack and his first bowl is round peg, as it would mean having to find the land without any previous indication. On round peg marks a bowl just short of the jack will be useful, forcing the player to bowl past it which could make him play through.

It is much safer on round peg marks to take more ground with the bowls than with the jack.

Marks

Although you can bowl anywhere on a crown green a player should not be tempted to move elsewhere when playing a particular mark and scoring consistently. An experienced bowler will take care not to show his opponent the other way to the jack, by sending his second bowl on the other bias (peg), unless his opponent has already delivered his two bowls.

On a round peg mark the bowl will turn more and more sharply as it slows down. How pronounced this arc is will depend on the steepness of the slope of the green, which in turn depends on the height of the crown. The nearer the crown that you play, the sharper will be the tendency of bowls to turn, with the reverse happening when you play further away from the crown.

A round peg mark normally depends on you delivering your bowls with the bias towards, rather than against the crown. If you are bowling on a green that slopes from right to left, and you send a bowl finger bias (for a right-hander) the natural tendency of the bowl to swing to the left will be increased by the degree of slope of the green.

Equally if you are bowling over a left to right slope, thumb bias will increase the swing to the right. Only on a green with a very high crown will you see round peg shots produced against the bias, these are known as falling marks.

Straight peg bowling is often defined in crown green circles as the beginners' peg. Certainly it is the easier peg to play because you don't need as much land as with round peg. It doesn't mean that you bowl directly at the jack because you will still get some movement from the bowl. Straight peg is played when the bias on your bowl will be facing the crown, the bowl fighting against the slope of the crown. Again, nearer the crown you will get cases where the bowl will fall against the bias on a falling mark.

The size of the slope does not matter, it's the angle of the slope that influences the bowl. Any ridges or hollows on the green's surface will also affect the bowls.

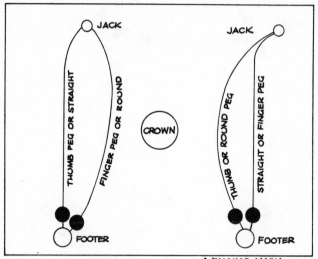

A STRONG ROUND PEG MARK   A FALLING MARK

Striking

There will be an occasion when you will want to do one of two things – either take out your opponent's bowl or take the bowl through. A through bowl is normally played when your opponent has had both his shots and is counting with a bowl fairly close to the jack.

When playing this shot you should remember that your weight should be for a bowl that would finish about three metres behind the jack if unimpeded in its travel. Therefore you would cut down on the amount of land – the shorter the length, the straighter your shot.

If you feel that your opponent holds a fairly un-beatable shot then you will play a striking bowl. This bowl will be played with considerable force as the faster your bowl travels the less it has a chance to deviate from its line.

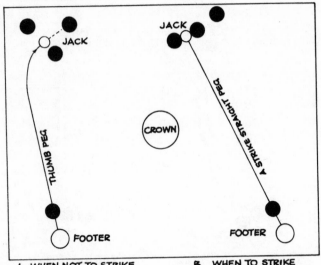

A. WHEN NOT TO STRIKE   **B. WHEN TO STRIKE**

Round peg striking has more chance of succeeding on the longer marks as it gives your bowl a wider hitting area than a straight peg strike. The longer the strike the more tolerance you have and a strike can also be played on a falling mark.

Chapter 5

How the game is played

The purpose of the game of bowls is to get your bowls closer to the jack than those of your opponent. One bowl nearer than your opponent's will give you one point, or 'chalk' as it is commonly called.

The number of points to be scored to win a match will have been determined before the start of the game, either 21-up, 31-up or even 41-up. Some events include a 'handicap' which is an allowance made to a player to give him an equal chance in a game against a stronger player.

The right to start a game is decided by the toss of a coin. The player throwing the jack is called the leader. On commencing a game the footer must be placed by the leader within three metres of the entrance to the green on either the right or left side and one metre from the edge.

To set a mark, the leader bowls the jack 19 metres or over from the footer. As long as the jack remains on the green and is over this distance it is a mark. Objection to a mark must be made verbally after the first bowl has come to rest.

If the jack is struck off the green the end is deemed to have been played. Play resumes one metre from the point where the jack left the green, the same player setting the mark. If the jack is impeded in its course or stops on the land of other players using the same green it must be returned, and if two jacks are bowled near the same place, the last one to come to rest must be returned. If the jack is displaced then the players must agree to its point of replacement, otherwise the end is void.

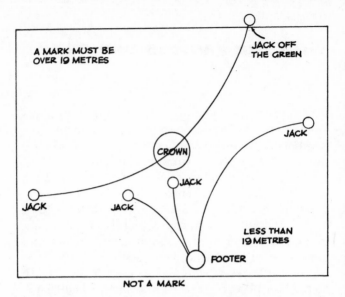

A MARK MUST BE OVER 19 METRES

JACK OFF THE GREEN

CROWN

JACK

JACK

JACK

JACK

LESS THAN 19 METRES

FOOTER

NOT A MARK

The end is also void if a player strikes the jack and it comes in contact with a bowl or jack not belonging to the game being played.

A bowl becomes dead if it travels less than 3 metres (3 yds 10 ins) from the footer; it is played or struck off the green; it falls from a player's hand, even by accident, and runs so far that it cannot be recovered without quitting the footer; if a player delivers an opponent's bowl by mistake.

After delivering a bowl a player must not approach within a metre of the running bowl, nor follow it up in such a way as to obstruct the view of his opponent. The player must not either try to accelerate or impede its progress. If a player offends the bowl can be taken out of play.

On the completion of each end the player with his bowl nearest to the jack will set the next mark. This is quite important for a player as it means he can continue to determine the length and type of mark – either short or into the corners.

Choosing a mark

All bowlers have their favourite marks, and likewise lengths that they don't perhaps find quite as well. So common sense dictates that as soon as they get the jack they will want to bowl to this favourite length.

This doesn't always apply, of course, as you will not want to reveal too much to your opponent. There is a certain amount of kidology included in the game – perhaps you might even play your known weakness to begin with to lull your opponent into a false sense of security. The best way to get over this is to become as competent as possible on all lengths.

Some bowlers may regard the footer as something of a fixture but you can use it when picking your aiming marks on the green. If when watching the jack while setting a mark it pegs two metres or so then aim two metres above the jack. Or on a falling mark the jack runs straight, then falls a metre or so at the end, play your bowl about a metre above the jack.

Remember it is easier to bowl using an aiming mark. For example if you are playing a round peg mark on a finger mark, then aim your first bowl about 5 cm (2 inches) above the mark, and if that is not enough increase it slightly with your second bowl. Obviously you go below when playing straight peg but don't allow as much when you are playing a falling mark because the weight of your own bowl will help to compensate for the difference in strength.

Changing pegs

A bowl will give you a good idea as to what to do when you change peg if you have a basic knowledge of a bowling green. Whatever angle you are to the crown, you can relate the slope of the green whether it is for or against you, when playing the other peg.

That doesn't mean to say that you can guarantee getting a close bowl, but many times you will only

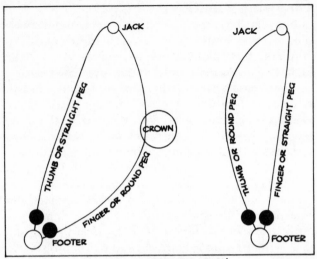

MARK ACROSS THE GREEN

need to get within a metre of the jack to count for another shot.

A round peg shot tells you a lot in its last two metres – the more the bowl pegs then it becomes obvious that a straight peg will have a vicious fall, if the round peg shot had a tendency to peg towards you. If the round peg shot shows a strong curved finish then it is a falling mark, which is not very vicious when playing straight peg.

It's only on a round peg when on its finish it runs 'straight' that you know when changing your peg that there will be movement to the peg at the finish. It may fall on the way but the straight part of the round peg tells you that there should be movement to some degree at the finish of a straight peg bowl.

The less the movement at the finish of a round peg, the more movement you will get on a straight peg. On some bowling greens you will find marks that can be played with a round peg but your bowl will move only slightly in relation to a normal round peg. And when playing the so-called straight peg your bowl will in fact peg more than that of the round peg.

Variations in the bowls

It should not take you long to establish the strength of your opponent's bowls in relation to your own. After that you will want to play marks which are most beneficial to your bowls. This makes it just that much harder for your opponent. You can also use the footer to make the difference more pronounced.

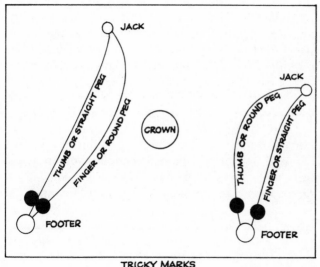

TRICKY MARKS

On any bowls green you will play on, there will be certain marks more suitable for either weak or strong biased bowls. With experience you will become aware which particular marks suit your bowls best and likewise where you are going to find problems.

If you have bowls with a weak bias, then it will not be wise to play close to the edges of the green where falling marks are most predominant, or close to the crown which normally produces the same characteristics.

Obviously what does not suit the weaker biased bowl will suit the stronger, so such marks can be played when you have a stronger biased bowl. Round peg bowling is more suitable for the player with the weaker biased bowl, as they will not wander far from the jack when played off-line as a stronger biased bowl would do following the same line. This is more pronounced when playing on a high crowned green where a stronger biased bowl could drift away from the jack, especially on top of a ridge.

If your bowls are stronger than the jack, or your opponent's bowls, it is advisable not to play long sweeping round peg marks, unless you can allow the required extra land and length involved in playing a line outside that of the jack.

The variations in bias because of the strength or weakness of a bowl also apply to bowls that have a different shaped sole. If you have a player using a narrow-soled bowl play him on falling marks because his bowls will have a tendency to slip away from such marks. If playing with a broad-soled bowl then a short straight mark will be easier to find.

Chapter 6

Outdoor greens and how to read them

A bowling green is like an open book, it is there to be read and understood. Whatever green you may encounter, a careful study of it can often help you to improve your game. Don't just stand and observe by the side of the green, walk over it. Look to see where the crown of the green is – they're not all in the centre – and see how high it is. Look for places that are likely to run heavy and for places at the edges where a bowl is likely to run away sharply.

When the crown is in the dead centre of the green then you can usually expect it to run faster two ways and slightly heavier on the other two. Often this will apply to the corners as well.

It is as well to weigh up the surrounds of the green as they often give a clue to the general lie of a green. A green where the surrounds slope away sharply will often have one side of the green which runs away a little as well. Paths and hedges can also supply clues to how level a green is. If they slope a little one way, it's odds on that the green will as well.

This is, of course, only a rough guide and sometimes the green will lie quite opposite to its surroundings – but it gets you into the habit of making observations and becoming more expert at analysing the greens contours.

If a green has an off-centre crown then it follows that one side of the green will have a longer slope than the other. It is highly likely that this will be the faster side when bowling over it, but you will need to push your bowls more when bowling into it.

The flatter the crown on the green, the more difficult in general it becomes to read. The crown in itself really gives nothing away. Once again though it will help to look for any 'hills and hollows' on the green.

Sometimes you will play on greens that have been laid on areas dug out on slopes and they can be the most confusing. Take a green that has been laid on a hillside. The side facing the hill can often be the heavier side and give the impression of sloping upwards.

Trees surrounding a green can often play a part in how the green runs. During the spring and summer months when they are in full leaf they will cast shadows over the green shielding the sun. This will keep the green moist and therefore heavier. The closer the trees are to the green, the more this occurs, especially as evening falls.

Look around the green for lighter and darker patches of grass and moss. The darker patches will tend to be heavier and show where moisture tends to hold. Where the grass is longer will indicate a hollow in the green as the cutting blades of the mower have not been able to quite reach.

Take a good look at the edges of the green all round, up to about four metres in. See if the slope is more pronounced on any of the edges. Obviously the greater the slope, the greater the tendency for a bowl to run away.

Finally take a look at the way the grass is cut. Remember that the more grass there is on a green, the heavier it will run. You must also remember that when a green is cut with panels going in opposite directions, one panel – that where the mower has been travelling the same way that you are preparing to bowl – will be faster than that of the one in the opposite direction.

One of the harder types of green to bowl on is that

which seems to be on a twist, as every bowl seems to run to one corner and there can be a vast difference in speeds going one way to another. But these are the very greens that you have to master. To the home player they are a tremendous advantage, because he need only be an average player to give a really good player a hard time. However, it often does also mean that you don't have to get so close to the jack to take shot. The home player will obviously use the green to his best advantage. He will take you on round pegs and falling marks, which will challenge your skill to the utmost.

When playing a match on your own green it is as well to realise what advantages you have over your opponent. If he is a newcomer, then you will be able to exploit your knowledge of the green fully, but you must also remember that he may be an experienced campaigner who has been to your green several times before and knows the 'lie of the land'.

However, you still have the main advantage as quite often all he will remember is that it is usually heavy or fast and what areas are the best to bowl. In other respects you can still regard him as a stranger. It is your job to outwit your opponent on the trickier marks on the green and make his task in trying to beat you as difficult as possible.

On most marks there are two ways to the jack – one thumb, the other finger, but the home player should always try to exploit the hard way in – that is the longer-swinging round peg. It may be that you are happier on straight marks, but your opponent is also more likely to find these, than the more difficult round-peg marks.

As with most things, there are exceptions, and one to look for is the player with weak bowls who can often be exploited by the use of falling marks.

Another important consideration is that of keeping your opponent moving. Even if you are doing particularly well on a mark, don't stay on it too long because he will soon be able to find it as well. Try and show him as much of the green as possible and employ variations in length. In this way your opponent never really gets the chance to settle and will always be searching to get a consistent length.

You will encounter a lot of different greens and often the trickiest are in areas where mining has taken place. But remember that one of the delights of the game is finally cracking a difficult green.

It would seem then that the dice are heavily loaded against the away player, but it doesn't mean that he can't apply a winning strategy of his own. If you can get away with playing simple straight marks to begin with and get a few chalks on the score card, this will give you an early advantage. Try to stick to the same patch of green as long as possible. There is nothing like a few shots in the bag to build a player's confidence, and if you are feeling in form then there is no reason why you shouldn't succeed away from your own green. Try to keep away from the difficult marks, but if this doesn't work then try marks that the home bowlers avoid themselves. The chances are he isn't so hot on those marks either. Try some close to the edges of the green – usually straight or falling marks.

One mark it is best to avoid is one that is nearly always adjacent to the clubhouse or changing pavilion. It's often a fact that this is a mark that the home bowlers will know very well. Bowlers tend to have a little bit of a lazy streak in them and rather than carry their bowls all the way across the green they will 'bowl for the hut', often with a little wager on the side.

Possibly the hardest art to master, but one that will give you most satisfaction, is bowling on a very fast green. Here your grip will need to be at its most gentle, the action of delivery coming more from the fingertips and not from the arm as on the heavier greens.

You will take a much shorter stride off the mat and cut down on the movement of your backswing. The weight of your bowl will have a great deal of influence on the game – the heavier bowls will run on so much more on the glass-like surface where even the jack has a battle to stay on. It may pay in these cases to avoid playing too close to the edges of the green and remember that any bowl going over the crown will gather speed on the other side.

Chapter 7

Mental approach and concentration

At the start of any chapter on the right way to approach playing a game it is as well to stress that there is no substitute for good practice. However good a bowler is, he needs to become as proficient as he can if he intends to succeed. The bowler who just wants to go out and enjoy himself and has no aspirations won't bother, but those who do want to succeed must practise.

Concentrate on improving your weaknesses and bowl at what you consider your most vulnerable length. Another good method is to play a mark round peg with your first bowl and straight peg with your second. This is also one of the quickest ways to learn how to play that green if you vary your length and try all marks on the green. When changing from round to straight peg, remember to take some weight, or running, off and vice versa.

Don't stick to a particular length if you suddenly find that you can play it well. There is the danger that while you may get an expert at this length, you will tend to struggle when bowling a different length. Always try to play the corners as well as the short marks.

A battle of wits

Bowls, like most games, is a battle of wits and particularly in singles play it is two players trying to weigh up their opponent and then trying to outmanoeuvre and master him. But one point a bowler must always remember is never to be frightened by reputations. Many a top-class bowler has been beaten by a so-called novice. Always adopt the attitude that your opponent is just another player and never let reputations frighten you.

Always remember that the best way to improve your game is by playing against the top players and that there is always something to learn even in defeat. Watching them as well as playing them can also improve your game. They have reached the top because they are good.

Slow-starters and front-runners

In bowls there are what are termed 'slow starters' and 'front-runners'. Quite simple terms and self-explanatory. The front-runners tend to play brilliantly in the opening stages and you think that they are going to overwhelm you.

In this case you must be patient enough to hold on and fight back because you will usually find that as you begin to whittle their lead away they suddenly become more human and the bowls that were finishing so close to the jack are now beginning to go through or be short.

Never let the front-runner demoralise you. Equally, never get too complacent when playing a slow-starter. You may get an early advantage, but do not allow yourself to be lulled into a false sense of security, as your opponent may suddenly strike when you are least expecting it. This type of player often struggles early in the game, but comes into his element in the dangerous latter stages. Remember, you can lose a game 21–20, as well as 21–0. One consolation is that in aggregate team games it is better to win by the highest possible margin, or alternatively to lose by the lowest.

Nerves

One of your biggest opponents on the game is something that you must master – nerves. If you are a player that doesn't suffer from nerves, then you obviously have a big advantage, although it helps to get the adrenalin flowing if you feel a little tense at the start of a match.

But it is important to maintain your concentration and competitive edge at all times, particularly at crisis points. It is here that the player must keep his nerve. If he goes to pieces, control of line and length can go out of the window.

When you meet a top-class player, remember that the onus will be on him to do well because this is expected of him. You are the underdog and few expect you to win. So psychologically that's an advantage for a start.

A lot will depend on where the match is being played and what for. Obviously if it is a league match or the early rounds of a tournament, then some of the tensions surrounding big occasions will be missing. But nevertheless your approach should always be the same.

Naturally if you are playing in front of a big crowd, perhaps even a televised game, then further tensions will be added. You will be wanting to give your best performance so as not to let yourself and others down.

Those that do suffer from nerves do have a problem, so it's as well to try and conquer them as much as possible. Some players use a 'Job's comforter' to ease their tensions – like smoking a pipe. Others polish their bowls before each delivery. Non-smokers may chew gum – anything that helps you to concentrate and ease tensions. Whatever tool you use, if you can convince yourself that it helps – then it succeeds in doing its job.

Concentration

Concentrating on the task in hand is most important for any bowler if he wants to succeed. You must never be distracted by what's going on elsewhere. Some players adopt tactics which are designed to put you off – it's called by some gamesmanship. Try to ignore these tactics, or turn them to your advantage by being even more determined to win.

A common tactic employed by some is to make a noise just as you are about to deliver. He may whistle, cough even rattle bowls or even make some remark to you or a nearby player. It will always be accompanied by a quizzical expression, even an apology, as if it was never his intention to put you off! A gentle reminder to keep quiet while you are delivering, said in the most polite manner, can often cut this out.

Watch the person who stands too close to you during your delivery. He may do it unintentionally, but if he catches your eye it can be off-putting. Again a pleasant request to 'stand back a little' should be sufficient.

Some people have the habit of following bowls up the green. Some can't help it, it's built-in natural enthusiasm, but others do it to obstruct your view of the bowl, which is against the rules. Again a quick reminder to that player can be enough to stop him.

No matter how annoying it may be, never fight fire with fire, as you will be accused of poor sportsmanship yourself.

You will encounter some more off-putting tactics but you must try to put them to the back of your mind and keep your concentration at all times. Also never let the remarks of spectators and 'bank experts' put you off. Most of them know how to play far better than you – it's always easier to play from the sidelines!

Assessing the game

Often you will approach a match with a fairly fixed plan of campaign in your mind, although you will probably try to play your normal game.

You must quickly assess your opponent's strengths and weaknesses in the first few ends and try to keep to the marks that cause him the most difficulty. Never be put off bowling marks which you personally dislike if this is a mark which causes your opponent some difficulty.

If, however, your opponent seems quite adept at most marks, try to make the best use of the footer to try and break any consistency that he may have found. You can set about this by never standing on the footer in the same position when delivering a bowl. Obviously you would need to adopt the same position for both bowls on any one end, but you can create footwork variations in the land which you take and that of your opponent, which will make it difficult for him to follow your line. Your opponent can, of course, counteract this but if it succeeds in upsetting his rhythm enough to allow you to get an advantage then you have achieved your objective.

Many bowlers regard the footer as a fixture and only use it as the starting position for any end. But you are allowed to move the footer within a radius of a metre from where the jack finished at the termination of the previous end, so you can legitimately use this rule to your advantage.

If your strong point is playing along the edges of the green you can move the footer into a position which gives you a chance to exploit the strength or weakness of your bowls. This also applies to a mark which involves bowling along a ridge or in a hollow.

Watch the player, however, who just drags the footer a fraction away from its original position. If you don't notice it you may wonder why your bowl has wandered off line when you deliver again.

Right-handed and left-handed

It is always difficult for a player to play against an opponent who bowls with the opposite hand. It's like an orthodox boxer who stands with his left arm and left leg forward being faced with a southpaw opponent whose stance is the opposite.

You must realise that if you are right-handed, then you cannot follow the same land as a left-hander. It helps to stand on the extreme edge of the mat on your left to compensate to a certain degree for the difference in land. A rough judge is the width of your left-handed opponent's shoulders. You will have to narrow the land on the left-hander's finger peg, which is your thumb, but allow more land when he plays thumb. Take note how he stands and watch closely where he strides from the mat.

There is a very dubious practice of some bowlers known as 'cross-legging'. What happens is that on delivery a player, for this instance we will take a left-hander, crosses his left leg over his right and brings his arm diagonally towards his left on delivery. If you, a right-hander, followed the same line your bowl would act differently. The 'cross-leggers' main armament is the thumb peg and usually he will stand on the extreme right-hand edge of the footer if he intends to play this type of shot. It is fair to say, however, that the vast majority of players in this game play straight, although it's as well to know what you can come up against so that it does not put you off your game.

Luck

Win or lose you always gain some experience from a game. To be beaten by the sheer better ability of your opponent is never a disgrace. But there is also one other factor that comes in occasionally and you must learn to live with it – luck. It has often been said that bowls is ruled by three 'Ls' – land, length and luck.

Sometimes lady luck sits on your shoulder, sometimes on your opponent's. The main point is never to be put off when she smiles sweetly at your opponent. It must never damage your concentration. Some bowlers take the rubs of the green too hard, and end up losing confidence and blame every subsequent mistake on just one incident.

Remember that luck is something nobody has any control over and has to be accepted. It is never the complete cause of the winning or losing a game. What separates the better-class player from his fellow bowlers is consistency. The ability to play more bowls closer to the jack.

Chapter 8

Fault finding and correction

The bowl that always lets you down is a bad one. You are never going to completely eliminate it, but there are ways to try and ensure that it does not happen too often.

Apart from a couple of instances, players should never bowl short. You should always aim to reach the jack or a little beyond. Either of these two cases will get you shots, because short bowls rarely count unless helped on their way by an opponent or a heavier weighted bowl of your own. So a golden rule must be – 'never be short'!

Obviously any bowl past the jack gives your opponent a clearer view of the jack and sometimes it may pay you to put a bowl a little short and in his draw. It will form an obstruction and if he strikes it it will have the effect of playing your bowl up while probably stopping his. This type of bowl is often best a few metres short as it would tend to get in the opponent's field of vision. It does, however, give him a chance to draw round the bowl if he can master his weight.

Don't rush into playing a shot as this can result in a bad bowl and don't strike at the head with your first bowl, just because your opponent may have laid one on the jack. If you miss with your strike you have just given your opponent another chance to draw one more shot. This might be different if your opponent is holding game.

Never try to show your opponent the easy way to the jack. If he has played a bad bowl on a hard mark, don't change peg, beat him on the bad hand. A good bowl is not essential here to beat the bad bowl he played, a moderate one will get shot. While realising that the object is to get close to the jack, as long as you get shot – it's one on the scorecard.

However, if three bowls have been played on one hand and you are holding shot, then you can change peg and score a second. Why take the risk of perhaps playing your opponent up, when you hold shot.

Some players fall down because they think that you have to follow the jack line all the time. Remember to count in the game all you have to do is get nearer than your opponent.

When playing up to the edges always try to keep your second bowl on. Never give your opponent the opportunity, even if you are holding shot, of firing you off and scoring two by having a second in what was seemingly a non-scoring position. Get your second bowl in there somewhere.

Length bowling on a crown green is particularly important as with the possibility of diagonal marks the variations in length are increased. To become a top-class player you must be able to play all lengths. So 'always reach the jack' must remain the motto.

Beware of the player who can play what might seem a bad bowl, but has in fact been played wisely. A player who has great knowledge of a green might play what looks like a short bowl, but he has deliberately contrived to play it on to a ridge. You bowl past this short bowl and find yours running on, and on past the jack. This type of shot is often played on the fast, fiery greens. If you have previously inspected the green, you should have picked up the lie of the land to counteract this tactic.

Perhaps the main secret in improving your game and counteracting any faults that you may have picked up is to try and bowl naturally. Never rush your delivery and try to stay properly balanced.

During the course of a game you will probably play a bowl that didn't exactly follow the line of the jack, despite going over the same aiming mark as the jack. The ability to rectify your first bowl and produce the winner from your second shot, is one of the main factors towards good bowling.

How your bowl behaves can also have something to do with the type of bowl you have in comparison with the jack or the weight with which you played it.

If you followed the same line as the jack and your bowl finished on a perfect length but a metre to the right, then you would need to narrow the land for the second bowl by around a couple of centimetres or so. Do not vary the land too much as you may be bowling through a ridge which is causing the variation. Alter the land too much and your bowl will just finish wide on the other side of the jack.

One lesson to remember is that if an overplayed bowl finishes up narrow, it is highly likely that a better length will finish more narrow still. The swing will probably be more pronounced on a shorter length.

The shot, however, that often fools more bowlers than any other, is the one which is played about a metre through but stays about a metre wide. Often a player will narrow his land thinking that this was the fault and finish across the head from the jack. What he should do in this case is follow the same line and just drop his weight slightly. Don't alter the line of your second bowl unless you have played a good length with your first and it finished off line with the jack. It is only with being on the same line to the jack and having perfect length that will tell you that there is something tricky about that mark.

Chapter 9

Other aspects of the game

Crown green bowling is basically an outdoor game covering the period from the end of March to about the middle of October but there are some aspects that are beginning to change.

Winter bowling

Winter bowling has opened up another avenue for the lesser-known bowlers to come in contact with the better-class player. Some of the top names now take advantage of the many winter events being run. It has meant that come rain, sunshine, snow or ice, the season never closes and that some greens only operate during the winter months, giving the summer greens a rest. Who would have thought that players could be wishing each other all the best for the festive season over Christmas while out on the green!

As the demand for winter bowling increases, more clubs will be tempted to provide greens for this bowling. The weather can obviously cause problems, but a surprising amount of enterprise has been shown to ensure that the greens are kept clear. Instances of JCB diggers being employed for snow clearance are not unheard of.

Players taking advantage of the winter bowling matches are always going to have the edge because they will always be in practice and will not have to spend time at the beginning of a new official outdoor season having to 'play themselves in' again.

The onset of early darkness outdoors during the winter months can, of course, be offset by the installation of flood-lighting which has already been done on some greens.

It is highly likely that winter bowling will gain new converts all the time.

Indoor bowling

There is another avenue for crown green bowlers to explore during the winter months, that of indoor bowling. At the moment this is mainly a flat green enterprise, although an indoor crown has been available at the Tranmere Rovers Football Ground for some time.

The Tranmere green was very much in the nature of an experiment and was first in its field, but the time is not so far off for the advent of a properly laid out indoor crown green.

Indoor bowling surface manufacturers have now perfected their carpets to suit most conditions and it is quite possible with concrete and screeding techniques to provide a crown surface. It need not be a really large crown, as an indoor surface will obviously run faster and truer than the outdoor grass.

This would certainly alleviate the main drawback to bowling outdoors in the winter, which is the unreliable weather conditions that we experience in the UK.

Bowls on television

There is no doubt that the advent of bowls on television has done much to bring many more players into the game, particularly the younger players. I think it's quite true to say that the days when bowls was considered purely a sport for older people have gone, because the television programmes have shown most clearly that the younger bowlers are coming through in top tournaments. BBC television played a big part in the early days with their Masters Tournament which later became a Pairs competition and now the independent stations have featured tournaments.

Even the most famous handicap of all, the Waterloo Autumn, has been covered on television and those who watched the 1982 final between Dennis Mercer of Cheshire and Ken Strutt of Oldham, witnessed one of the most exciting finals ever seen at Blackpool's Waterloo Hotel, with Mercer just getting home 21–20.

Professionals

Crown green has always had its professional aspects. The British Professional Bowling Association, commonly known as the Panel, runs matches under its auspices on scheduled greens with players selected by the association. At one time many top bowlers belonged to the panel but with the withdrawal of amateur status under British Crown Green Bowling Association rules there is now not so much need for such a body.

The British Bowls Professional Players Association was formed in 1982 to pursue the interests of the top bowlers with players invited to join who have proved themselves over the years to be the best. The association currently has 12 top players but plans to increase this number as and when the professional bowls game increases.

Bowls for everyone

Throughout this book there has been no mention of players being either male or female and that is deliberate because bowls is one of those sports that can be enjoyed by both sexes.

There are a lot of women playing crown green bowls and their numbers are on the increase. The British Crown Green Bowling Association is, however, run for the benefit of male bowlers, but their executive has always stated its willingness to help the ladies form their own association, similar to that of their flat green counterparts.

The women do have organised competitions to play for like the Ladies Waterloo and the Isle of Man tournament, and ladies leagues and county competitions are on the increase.

There is no doubt that as the game of bowls begins to complete a very widespread expansion in all areas of the UK in both crown and flat, that women's bowls will become every bit as important as men's. The only inhibiting factor being the embarrassment felt by some men at being beaten by a woman opponent.

Chapter 10

Laws of the game of crown green bowls

Printed by permission of the copyright holders, the British Crown Green Bowling Association

1. The game shall be played by two players, each having two bowls, the players playing alternately until each shall have delivered both bowls, except in the event of one player having forfeited his first bowl, in which case his opponent will then be allowed to deliver his two bowls consecutively. A bowl must be played at least three metres from the footer to count, except when an opponent's bowls are out of play. Before commencing play the number of points to be scored to make the game shall be fixed. (Where more than two players take part in a game, these Laws shall operate when applicable.) The entrance (which must be near the centre of any one side) shall be plainly marked.

2. Commencement of game
On commencing a game, the footer must be placed by the leader within three metres of the entrance to the green on either right or left side, and one metre from the edge, and from there play shall commence.

3. The jack
Standard jacks as defined in Appendix A shall be used in all competitions.

4. The footer
Every player must place his toe on the footer when bowling either jack or bowl. A player bowling the jack with his right hand must play his bowls with the right hand and must have his right toe on the footer, and a player bowling the jack with his left hand must

play his bowls with the left hand and must have his left toe on the footer. A player must bowl with the same hand throughout the game. Any bowl not so played may be stopped by the referee, and shall then be played again. If a player shall again transgress during the course of the game, the bowl wrongly played shall be deemed dead. A player may retain possession of the footer until his bowl has ceased running. The footer, which shall be round, shall have a diameter of not less than 128 mm (5 inches) and not more than 154 mm (6 inches). Nothing in this rule shall apply to any player who suffers a disability.

5. A mark

The leader shall bowl the jack to set a mark, the object of the players being to play their bowls as near as possible to the jack. To set a mark, the jack must be bowled and if it rests on the green at all (except as Law 7) it shall be deemed a mark.

6. Who shall set mark

If the leader in one trial shall fail to set a mark, his opponent is then entitled to set the mark with the same jack, but not to play first at it. If the opponent fails in one trial to set a mark, the original leader shall then have one trial, and so on alternately, until a mark has been set by one of them, the original leader to play the first bowl at it.

7. Not a mark

The following shall be deemed 'not a mark'. If, after objection, the jack is proved by measurement to be less than 19 metres from the footer, the measurement to be taken from the nearest point of the jack to the centre of the footer.

If, when bowled, the jack shall go off the green.

8. Objection to a mark

Objection to a mark must be made verbally after the first bowl has come to rest. Any player objecting to a mark must raise his hand as an indication to the referee that an objection has been made.

9. If (after objection to a mark has been made) it is proved by measurement to be a mark, the jack and bowl shall remain.

10. If the original leader fails to set a mark, and objects to the mark set by his opponent, he shall not be allowed to bowl his wood until the objection has been settled, and if the measurement shall prove that a legitimate mark has been set, it must be accepted.

11. A tape or other certified measure (at least 19 metres long) must be used for the purpose of carrying out these Laws.

12. Method of scoring

The winner of each end shall score one point for each bowl he has nearer to the jack than his opponent's nearest bowl, and he shall lead out the jack at the succeeding end. When measuring, the adjustable end of the pegs or permitted metal measures as approved by the British Crown Green Bowling Assocation must be taken to the jack. Only the winner of the end shall signal the result to the scorers who must sit together, and initial each other's score cards every third end to signify agreement.

13. Delivery of jack

A player shall not bowl the jack without allowing his opponent the opportunity of seeing with what bias he bowls it, and of watching its course from a point near the footer.

14. Jack struck off green

If the jack is struck off the green that end shall be deemed to have been played. Play shall resume one metre from the point where the jack left the green, the same player setting the mark.

15. Replacing footer

If a player shall have taken up the footer after playing a bowl, which for any reason has to be replayed, the footer shall be replaced as nearly as possible in its former position.

16. After each end is concluded, the footer shall be placed at the jack by the last player. The leader in the succeeding end may, however, before bowling the jack, remove the footer anywhere he pleases within the space of one metre from the spot where the jack lay at the termination of the preceding end.

17. Changing jack or bowls

No player shall be allowed to change the jack or bowls during the progress of a game except with the consent of the referee and then only if in his opinion the jack or bowls are so damaged as to be unplayable. No player shall be permitted to play with bowls or jack which have a device for adjusting the bias, nor shall any player be permitted to alter the bias of bowls or jack, by any means, during the course of play.

18. Jack impeded

If the jack in its course is impeded in any way, or stops on the land of other players, it must under all circumstances be returned, and if two jacks are bowled near the same place, the one that is last stationary must be pronounced not a mark and be returned, no penalty being incurred.

19. Jack displaced

If the jack is displaced by a bowl or the jack from any other players, or by any exterior cause, and the players agree as to the spot of replacement, the end must be continued, otherwise the end is void.

20. If a player strikes the jack with his bowl, and the jack comes into contact with a bowl or jack not belonging to the playing party, or if it comes in contact with any person on the green the end becomes void; but if the jack comes in contact with a bowl belonging to the playing party, it must remain at the place to which it is removed by the strike.

21. No player shall deliver a bowl while the jack or a preceding bowl is in motion, otherwise his bowl shall be deemed dead and must be taken out of play.

22. Approaching running bowl

A player must not approach nearer than one metre to a running bowl, nor follow it up in such a manner as to obstruct the view of his opponent. He must not endeavour to accelerate or impede its progress. If he offends the bowl shall be taken out of play and in the case of a further offence, his bowls shall be taken off the green and the game shall be awarded to his opponent, the defaulter's score at that point to count.

23. Playing out of turn or with a bowl other than own

If a bowl is played out of turn it must be returned and played again in its proper turn. If a bowl other than the player's own is delivered whether by mistake or otherwise, it shall be deemed a dead bowl to that player and be returned to the proper owner to be played, the defaulter losing one of his bowls as a penalty. If however, the jack or a bowl already played is disturbed by the bowl wrongly played, it shall be replaced as nearly as possible in its original position.

24. Running bowl impeded

If a running bowl is impeded in any way (except by either player), it must be played again. If a running bowl is impeded by either player, both the offending player's bowls shall be forfeited at the end concerned. If, however, the leader's first bowl is impeded, he may, if he so desires, have the jack returned to him to set another mark. If a running bowl comes into contact with the jack or any of the bowls in the set, such jack and/or bowls must remain where they stop.

25.

When, after delivery of the jack and a mark is set, the leader is prevented from delivering his first bowl through the tape being on the green during the measure of another mark, the leader may have the jack returned and again set the mark.

26.   Jack or bowl in danger of striking still bowl or jack

If a running jack or bowl appears to be in danger of striking a still bowl or jack belonging to another set, such running jack or bowl should be stopped and returned to be replayed.

27.   Disturbing a still bowl

If a still bowl is disturbed by any person other than the players concerned, or by a bowl or jack of any other players, it must be replaced as near as possible to its original position, but should either player touch or displace a still bowl before the end is completed, both the offending player's bowls shall be forfeited at the end concerned.

28.   Moving jack or bowls before opponent agrees

At the conclusion of an end, neither the jack nor a bowl claimed to count may be moved without the consent of the opponent until the points are counted and both players are satisfied, otherwise the opponent shall score one point for each of his bowls in play. No measuring is permitted until the end is finished. In the event of the displacement of the jack during a measure the points already given shall stand.

29.   Bowl falling from player's hand

If a player has taken up his position, and a bowl falls from his hand (even by accident) and runs so far that he cannot recover it without quitting the footer, such bowl shall be considered dead and must be taken out of play.

30.   Blocking opponent's course

A player may play his bowl so as to block his opponent's course whenever he thinks proper, but he must not play his bowl a less distance than three metres from the footer, otherwise it shall be deemed dead and must be taken out of play. A bowl must be played, not placed, or it becomes a dead bowl.

31. Displacing jack or bowl during measure, bowl resting on another

If, during a measure, the jack or bowl is displaced by a player, he shall lose the point claimed. When a bowl rests on another, or is touching the jack, and the bowl rested on has to be removed to allow a measure it must be removed by the referee and the measure made after such removal.

32. Instructions to referees and measurers

The referee or measurer is not permitted to place either his thumb or fingers on either the jack or bowl when measuring an end.

33. Dead bowls

A bowl or jack played or struck off the green or prevented going off by resting against anything at the edge or in the channel, shall be dead.

34. Refusal or inability to continue game

If, after commencing a game, any player shall refuse or is unable to continue, the referee shall decide on the point at issue. Should a player leave the green without informing his opponent and obtaining the permission of the referee, he shall forfeit the game. Any incident which necessitates a player having to stop play or leave the green and is unable to resume before the finish of the match, his opponent shall receive the maximum points and the score of the player who left the green to remain as it stood.

35. No instructions permitted

Players or spectators must not instruct or give any intimation whatever to players when on the green.

36. No person, other than the players and the referee, are allowed on the green (except measurers when their services are required).

37. A player, when at the end where the jack lies, must not stand directly behind the jack or obstruct the view of his opponent.

38. Ungentlemanly conduct

In case of wilful breach of the Laws of the Game or

any unfair play or ungentlemanly conduct, the referee may caution the offending players or spectators or order them to retire from the game or green, and, if a player, no substitute shall be allowed to take his place. The game shall be awarded to his opponent, and the offending player's score at that stage shall count.

39. Bad light and postponement of game

If, during the course of a game, it becomes so dark that the jack cannot be distinctly seen from the footer, any player may have a light exhibited at the jack if he so requests, or he may appeal to the referee, whose decision shall be final, for the game to be postponed. In the event of a postponement, owing to the above cause or any other unforeseen circumstances the points scored by each player shall count and the position of the jack shall be marked.

40. Referee not to wait for an objection

Referees are instructed to insist on and see that the games are carried out strictly in accordance with the Laws of the Game.

41. Alteration of laws

The British Crown Green Bowling Association is the interpreter of these Laws, and from its decision there shall be no appeal either at Law or otherwise. None of these Laws shall be altered except as provided by the Association's Bye-Laws numbered 16 to 17 for the alteration of Rules and Bye-Laws.

42. Dispute not provided for in laws

Any dispute arising which is not provided for in the foregoing Laws, shall be decided by the referee whose decision shall be final.

New bowling greens

Following discussion on the construction of crown bowling greens the Association recommends that the height of the crown on a 36.5 × 36.5 metre (40 yards × 40 yards) green should be 30.5 cm (12 inch) and pro-rata on greens of other sizes.

Appendix A: a standard jack

1. Standard jacks of 2 Full bias as approved by the British Crown Green Bowling Association and the British Parks Bowling Association respectively, shall weigh a minimum of 567 gms (20 oz) and a maximum of 652 gm (23 oz) and the diameter shall be a minimum of 95 mm (3¾ in) and a maximum of 98 mm (3⅞ in). They shall be black in colour with white mounts and spots or white in colour with black mounts and spots. In place of mounts, composition jacks may have engraved circles of approximately the diameter of the mounts or spots and filled in the appropriate colour.

2. The mounts shall be approximately 20 mm (¹³⁄₁₆ in) diameter and bias side mounts shall not be hollow. The spots shall be approximately 6 mm (¼ in) diameter and there shall be three spots on the non-bias side at a radius of approximately 19 mm (¾ in) from the centre of the mount.

3. They shall not be numbered or lettered. Evidence of ownership shall be made on the non-bias side.

4. They shall be branded BCGBA and the Code letter of the Official Tester. All new standard jacks shall bear the manufacturer's name.

5. New and renovated jacks shall be stamped with the year of expiry and for this purpose the year shall be reckoned from 1 October to 30 September the next year (i.e. jacks manufactured or re-tested between 1 October and 31 December will bear the stamp of expiry from the following year). All jacks shall be re-tested at not more than seven yearly intervals.

The following Companies are the official appointed and only recognised Standard Jack Makers and Bias Testers to the British Crown Green Bowling Association.

Thomas Taylor (Bowls) Ltd., Glasgow	Letter A
The Premier Bowls Co., Stockport	Letter C
Taylor Rolph Co. Ltd., Penshurst	Letter D
Ellis-Birch Co., Manchester	Letter E
John Jaques & Sons, Thorton Heath, Surrey	Letter H
Composition Billiard Ball Supply Co., London	Letter J
Thomas Royle Ltd., Manchester	Letter K
Crown Sports Ltd., Dewsbury	Letter L
K. & S. Ltd., Chester	Letter M
E. A. Clare & Son, Liverpool	Letter X
A. F. Ayers Ltd., Liverpool	Letter Y

No. 2 full bias standard jacks

Prior to 1981 the No. 2 Full Bias of the Standard Jack has varied slightly from district to district and from one manufacturer to another and although they were in close proximity it is obvious that it would be beneficial to players and the Companies concerned to establish a definite Standard No. 2 Full Bias BCGBA Crown Green Jack.

The representatives of the Companies invited Officials of our Association to meet and discuss the matter.

Following talks exploring all aspects, stringent table tests of various specimen jacks were undertaken followed by green testing by representatives of the BCGBA. A satisfactory conclusion was reached and agreement made between the two bodies.

The benefit to be derived from the Agreement is that should any individual, Club, League or Association purchase new Standard Jacks or send existing jacks for testing, stamping and/or renovation to any of the appointed Companies and are later doubtful as to the trueness of the bias of such jacks they can be tested against their own Association 'Copy' jack and if still in doubt against the Master jack.

With re-test and date stamping of existing Standard jacks now required at not more than seven yearly intervals it will take time to eliminate variations but as jacks become due for re-test they will be returned complying with the specifications required or rejected as below standard.

Within reasonable time the arguments relating to weak/strong jacks will be eliminated and no matter where a bowler plays he at least can be sure than an officially stamped jack will be of true No. 2 Full Bias. The Secretary of the BCGBA holds the Master Jack, each County Association, Manufacturer and Bias Tester have exact copies of the Master Jack.

The Manufacturers and Testers have given an undertaking not to stamp any Standard Jack which does not conform to the weight, size and bias of a Standard Jack as specified in Appendix A of the Laws of the Game as published in the BCGBA Official Handbook.

Fixtures

Date   **Venue**

....
....
....
....
....
....
....
....
....
....
....
....
....
....
....
....
....
....
....
....
....
....
....
....
....
....
....
....